ATOMINERAL EXPLORATIONS

ISBN: 978-1-989940-12-9
© 2020 Jeremy Stewart
All rights reserved

Dimensionfold Publishing
Prince George
dimensionfold.com

ATOMINERAL EXPLORATIONS

Jeremy Stewart

affirmation affixed to being   whether with

or without poetry   folly rose

asocial pleasure in the recording   one

       hand immersed in the creek at all times

            the same in dreams

asyndeton   creek banks   between two

sites could become physical metaphorical material

devoid of natural meaning and realistic assumptions

atopos   poem against the sky of page's leaf

becoming entirely covered by forest

being a provisional theory of non-sites a flooded creek

        building a burning building   for thousands

of years   although now they have almost

entirely disappeared

cutting of the text   the father is reduced to the

name of the father   polyvocality

death rose high from the blue twilight of the valley

and clambered up the steepest slopes

difference   the line dividing what we can perceive

from what no one has ever yet seen   a starlit

path flanked by a small forest

dissociated   from drifting   their green

parasols   seem to float

dream-reading an asocial topic   untouched

   it's a kind of mathematics of desire

drift   for earth art   a dreamlike scent

   the stands of trees spared longest were those in

the most inaccessible regions   places the

creek won't reach

else   cloud pink   to depthless night

           remembered image came into my mind of a

forest   I understand less by the minute

           sometimes swans and herons

empty   travel in this space is a vast metaphor

envelope instead instead instead   that

rose   speaks to enclosure   its own

language, a closed system   daughter of a miner

killed in the Andromeda mines

           darkness on all sides

even theories   like all things   are eventually

abandoned   alps in the creek

where there used to be some houses   from

all the way across

figure   this three-dimensional metaphor

     one site represents another without

resemblance   from time to time I heard the

sounds of words   the figural points in all possible

machinic directions

fissure as invented   ulcerated   one

might call it a non-trip to a site from a non-site

follows without end   on the more level surfaces at

the head of the pass   cause of sleep

gleam of daylight faded   as the floodwaters rose

against and then   leaves glisten with a misting of

rain   someone has opened the door

         soft white shoes have been placed on the feet

of the little boy

harrowing arrows fall, we are told, like rain

          a crumpled page smoothed, crumpled,

smoothed again

homestead   Buckhorn Lake Road

imaginary   a three-dimensional picture which

doesn't look like a picture   if a shadow could cast

its own shadow

interior   a few forests of trees towering far taller

than those of today remain

intractable on overshadowed slopes and in ravines

joker   vacuous like night   press for phosphenes

        mint candy is blue   his posture resembled a

zelkova tree being blown over by the wind

knife   showed against the black heights

        undo grief

letter this language of sites   might always not

arrive   lying in a deep, cup-like hollow

limit-text must be masked by another kind of death

    melted black telephone   cedar rises

from where cedar fell

margin this park-like setting

necessary clouds bound the horizon of difference

before more rain   and from all these low-

growing plants rose the grey trunks   and the voices

    the darkness that had been retreating was

returning

non-site as the site of a site reproduced in a poem

    (an indoor earthwork)

a three-dimensional logical picture

outside it was still raining	abstract, yet it
represents an actual site	open like a
non-delimited collection	when I leave here
outside the sentence	between the actual site
and the non-site	exists a space of metaphoric
significance	with the creek beyond

pattern coming closer and closer to the rocky peaks

      every dream has two readings   white

floral print

precarious slender conifers which cannot be imagined

      stars began to show above the mountains

      eradicated almost without a trace today

quiet

reservoir the rain falls steadily

  stippling the water   lilac and blue

  turns desire against itself

return to such devastated places as strip mines then he

turned his eyes back onto the creek

ribbon   the dead animals

    the shrouds were transformative

  flown in by crashed helicopter

sentence   outlines of plants glowing in that
flickering light phosphenes for phonemes   no-site
of flightless bird   blindsighted by wildfires

shift   logical intuition   develop an
entirely new sense of metaphor free of natural or
realistic expressive content   smoked out if
you got 'em

site   the ground under these meager pines is largely
bare   the creek runs over a flat mountain
        burial in the sky

stage ghosts rework a ground plan or set diagram

       a forest of pencils   the walk into the rain

with their heavy packs on their backs   bathed

in light, floating across last words of the pilot

subtraction of one dimension to topologize

       in the end, night comes   drops at that

point from the ravine   drains the creek with a

portable hole

tears cut the statue a marble face   violet

to purple in colour   the house with the long

driveway   the house that was moved

tends left, mends, tenderly leaves leaves and needles

tmesis in the tear between the shedding of two tears

the site of the house that burned

unable   dialectic between mining and land

reclamation   I should discard   looking out the

windshield of a car   wipers on high

     rain streaming down   driving along a

one-lane road surrounded by a forest

undone   this theory is tentative and could be

abandoned at any time

vast theories compose the strata of many forgotten

books

withdrawn to drown in cloud mountain

     drawing a diagram, logic's two-dimensional

picture   scent of roses

writing differs from a natural or realistic picture in
that it rarely looks like the thing it stands for

    eyes on the sky

written now long since extinct   transfigured on
the last page

xylograph page cut by pencil   made up of
bells and xylophone   harps

    notebook as non-site   non-sitebook

    tunnel vision

yes

zelkova tree   a rose above all   a two-dimensional metaphor—A is Z

ATOMINERAL EXPLORATIONS is an abecedarian assemblage whose words are drawn from cuttings from *The Pleasure of the Text* by Roland Barthes; "A Provisional Theory of Non-Sites" by Robert Smithson; *Campo Santo* by W.G. Sebald; *A Night on the Galactic Railroad* by Kenji Miyazawa; *Pedro Paramo* by Juan Rulfo; and *The Anti-Oedipus Papers* by Felix Guattari. The rest of the text is from my own notebooks. ATOMINERAL EXPLORATIONS is set in Bodoni type.

Many thanks to Erin, Ephraim, and to Cesárea; to Robert Keith; to Ryan Fitzpatrick; to Annie Ginn; and to Ken Goudsward and Dimensionfold.

Jeremy Stewart

Surrey, BC, December 2020

jeremystewart.ca

www.ingramcontent.com/pod-product-compliance
Lightning Source LLC
Chambersburg PA
CBHW021433070526
44577CB00001B/185